THE FALL OF TAMMY SYTCH: FROM PRO WRESTLING STAR TO PRISONER

John A. Anderson

TABLE OF CONTENTS

INTRODUCTION

SUMMARY

CHAPTER 1: WHO IS TAMMY SYTCH
1:1 RISE TO NOTORIETY
1:2 BEGINNINGS OF PROFESSIONAL WRESTLING CAREER
1:3 ASCENT TO FAME
CHAPTER 2: REVEALED OF PERSONAL ISSUES
2:1 DIFFICULTIES OUTSIDE OF THE RINGS
2:2 INFLUENCE ON TAMMY SYTCH'S PRIVATE LIFE: AN UNCOVERED JOURNEY

CHAPTER 3: DECLINE IN CAREER
3:1 CHANGE IN WRESTLING TRAJECTORIES
3:2 WORKPLACE FAILURES
CHAPTER 4: UNREST IN THE LAW
4:1 NEW LEGAL CONCERNS: TAMMY SYTCH'S DISSECTING LEGAL ENVIRONMENT
4:2 DISSECTING THE IMAGE
Tammy Sytch's Journey Beyond Wrestling Stardom: Dissecting a Reputation
CHAPTER 5: THE CRITICAL JUNCTURE
5:1 IMPORTANT OCCURRENCES THAT CAUSE CHANGE

5:2 IMPORTANT MILESTONES IN SYTCH'S LIFE

CHAPTER 6: LIFE IN PRISON

6:1 DETENTION

6:2 REALITIES:

6:3 GETTING BY WHILE CONFINED

CHAPTER 7: CONTEMPLATING A LOST HERITAGE

7:1 LEGACY OF WRESTLING DIMINISHED

7:2 INTROSPECTIVE THOUGHT

7:3 INTROSPECTIVE ANALYSIS

CHAPTER 8: EFFORTS TO FIND ATONEMENT

8:1 REHABILITATION AFTER PRISON

8:2 TRYING TO MAKE A RETURN

CONCLUSION:

EPILOGUE: TEACHINGS ENGRAVED IN THE RING OF LIFE: A LEARNED EXAMPLE

REPERCUSSIONS: TAMMY SYTCH'S EFFECT ON THE WRESTLING World

INTRODUCTION

Few tales in the turbulent world of professional wrestling capture the highs and lows of celebrity and personal hardship like Tammy Sytch's. Her path from renown to notoriety took an unexpected turn after she was once hailed as a pro wrestling star. "The Fall of Tammy Sytch: From Pro Wrestling Star to Prisoner" explores the gripping story of a once-respected individual whose life outside of the ring turned into a string of difficulties related to both personal and legal issues.

This investigation reveals the intricacies of achievement, the influence of inner demons, and the unanticipated outcomes that finally brought Tammy Sytch from the glittering heights of the wrestling arena to the brutality of life in prison. Join us as we explore the complexities of a fallen star's life, looking at the aftermath of a legacy forever changed and attempting to comprehend the influences that determined her destiny.

Context

In the 1990s, Tammy Sytch—better known by her ring name, "Sunny"—became a notable figure in the professional wrestling industry. She was born in Matawan, New Jersey, on December 7, 1972. Her captivating personality and obvious skill helped her rise to the top of the wrestling world.

Throughout her early career, Sytch made a big impression on several wrestling companies. She was most successful during her time in the World Wrestling Federation (WWF), which is now known as WWE. She was a key figure in raising the popularity of various wrestling superstars as a valet and manager.

But underneath the glitter and splendor of professional wrestling, Sytch struggled with issues that would ultimately cloud her once-famous career. Her professional accomplishments started to take a backseat due to struggles with drug misuse, legal troubles, and turbulent relationships. This was the beginning of a downhill spiral that would reshape her legacy.

"The Fall of Tammy Sytch" delves into the intricate tale of a lady whose journey goes beyond the squared circle, exposing the difficulties associated with being famous, inner demons, and the harsh reality of life outside of the limelight. By delving into this story, we expose the many factors that led to Tammy Sytch's downfall and encourage introspection on the complex relationship between personal struggles, public perception, and success.

SUMMARY

"The Fall of Tammy Sytch: From Pro Wrestling Star to Prisoner" follows the fascinating journey of one of professional wrestling's luminaries, Tammy

Sytch, whose trajectory reflected both the heights of her fame and the depths of her inner struggle.

The book offers a thorough examination of Sytch's ascent to fame in the World Wrestling Federation (WWF) in the 1990s, when her charm and aptitude for management elevated her to a pivotal position in the wrestling world. As the story progresses, it dives into the emotional issues that eventually eclipse her professional accomplishments, ranging from drug misuse issues to legal entanglements.

The story revolves around the crucial event that precipitated Sytch's downfall, exploring the deep effects of legal issues and personal struggles on her professional wrestling career as well as her personal life. After that, the book delves into the harsh reality of Sytch's existence in prison, providing a complex account of her interactions with the legal system.

"The Fall of Tammy Sytch" aims to provide readers with a thorough knowledge of the causes that molded Sytch's path by illuminating the complex connections between success and hardship via painstaking research and intelligent writing. We encourage readers to consider the nuances of celebrity, the effects of one's own decisions, and the lasting impact on oneself and the wrestling community as we peel back the layers of this gripping story.

CHAPTER 1: WHO IS TAMMY SYTCH

Tammy Sytch, a.k.a. "Sunny" in the ring, is a personality, valet, and former professional wrestling manager. She was born in Matawan, New Jersey, on December 7, 1972, and rose to popularity in the wrestling industry in the 1990s. Sytch's tenure with the World Wrestling Federation (WWF), now known as WWE, is largely responsible for her rise to stardom.

She managed and escorted different wrestlers to the ring, becoming one of the first well-known female managers in the wrestling business. Sunny became well-known because of her personality, presence on television, and marketing prowess. However personal problems tainted her career, including drug use and legal challenges, which eventually caused her status in the industry to deteriorate.

The difficulties in Sytch's life outside of the ring—including stints in jail due to legal issues—attracted attention. She became a complicated character in the history of professional wrestling despite her early success in the business. Her career was one of highs and lows.

1:1 RISE TO NOTORIETY

Tammy Sytch's meteoric rise to fame in professional wrestling was characterized by her natural ability, charm, and key positions held by the World Wrestling Federation (WWF) in the middle of the 1990s.

1. **Early Breakthroughs:** Sytch's career started with her stunning ringside valet and manager appearance in Smoky Mountain Wrestling (SMW),

which drew in wrestling fans. Her early success paved the way for a bigger part on a more significant platform.

2. **Transition to the WWF:** The WWF accepted Sytch into its ranks after seeing her ability. She made a huge stride toward celebrity with this change, and she soon rose to prominence within the company.

3. **Managing High-Profile Teams:** After taking on management duties for well-known tag teams like The Bodydonnas, Sytch's career took off. Her leadership abilities helped these teams succeed, establishing her as one of the industry's most successful managers.

4. **Creative stories and Mic Skills:** In addition to her managerial abilities, Sytch's success stemmed from her participation in creative stories and her keen mic skills. The wrestling experience gained additional entertainment value from her skill at

capturing the audience's attention with captivating stories and well-spoken promos.

5. Female Trailblazer: Sytch broke gender stereotypes in professional wrestling by becoming one of the first well-known female managers. Her accomplishment demonstrated that executive positions were not just reserved for male achievers, and it opened doors for more women to enter the field.

6. Popularity and Merchandising: The WWF took advantage of Sytch's marketability as her popularity skyrocketed. Her appearance in advertising campaigns, merchandising, and promotional materials cemented her place as a well-known figure in the world of professional wrestling.

7. Mainstream Recognition: Professional wrestling was becoming more and more accepted in society at the same time as Sytch was rising to prominence. Her influence went beyond the world of professional wrestling, garnering interest from the general media and adding to the industry's increasing public awareness.

During her rise to prominence, Tammy Sytch broke down boundaries and had a lasting influence on the wrestling profession. She made dramatic contributions to the wrestling story. But as her profession developed, personal struggles grew entwined with it, changing the course of her legacy.

1:2 BEGINNINGS OF PROFESSIONAL WRESTLING CAREER

Tammy Sytch's entry into the professional wrestling business in the late 1980s was a defining moment in her early career. Her captivating personality and charismatic entrance into the wrestling industry would quickly make her stand out.

1. Tammy Sytch's Early Days and Training: She trained under seasoned wrestling professionals to start her career in the sport. Her commitment to the sport and her excitement for it were immediately apparent, setting the stage for her future aspirations.

2. Debut in Smoky Mountain Wrestling (SMW): In the early 1990s, Sytch made her professional wrestling debut via Smoky Mountain Wrestling (SMW). As a ringside valet, she created an impression by going with wrestlers and positioning herself as a manager.

3. Managerial Prowess at SMW: In her role as manager at SMW, Sytch demonstrated her aptitude for attention-grabbing and promotion. Her captivating personality and lively ringside presence enhanced the overall entertainment value of the contests she competed in.

4. The transition to the World Wrestling Federation (WWF): occurred because of Sytch's skill, which quickly drew the organization's attention. She underwent a major career shift when she joined the WWF, and by the mid-1990s, she was a key player in the promotion.

5. Managerial Role in WWF: Sytch kept showcasing her managerial skills in the WWF. She was the manager of several well-known wrestlers, including The Bodydonnas, who under her direction captured the WWF Tag Team Championship.

6. Popularity and notoriety: Tammy Sytch earned broad notoriety and popularity in the WWF throughout her formative years. She became one of the most well-known female characters in professional wrestling because of her on-screen charisma and her capacity to assume important roles in the plots.

Tammy Sytch's early career demonstrated both her management abilities and her capacity to hold an audience's attention, which served as a foundation for her rise to fame. But as her career developed, she faced personal difficulties that shaped the intricate story that would eventually come to define her reputation in the wrestling community.

1:3 ASCENT TO FAME

The combination of Tammy Sytch's natural charm, management skill, and an acute sense of audience engagement propelled her to popularity in the professional wrestling industry. Her rise to fame took place in the World Wrestling Federation (WWF) in the middle of the 1990s.

1. Charismatic Presence: From the beginning of her profession, Sytch stood out due to her captivating personality and lively demeanor. She rose to prominence in the wrestling business mostly due to her ability to engage the audience in her duties as a manager and on-screen.

2. WWF Debut and Managing The Bodydonnas: Tammy Sytch made a big impression when she signed up with the WWF and became the manager of The Bodydonnas, a tag team that included Tom Prichard and Chris Candido. The Bodydonnas were successful under her direction and won the WWF Tag Team Championship.

3. Creative Storylines and Mic Proficiency: Sytch's role went beyond overseeing in-ring performers. She also cemented her position as a key character in the wrestling narrative by contributing tales that showcased her razor-sharp humor and command of the microphone.

4. Marketing and Promotion: The WWF took advantage of Sytch's fame by showcasing her prominently in marketing campaigns after realizing her promotional worth. Using her picture to advertise events and items highlighted her importance to the company.

5. Women in Wrestling: Sytch was instrumental in dispelling gender preconceptions in the business as one of the first well-known female managers in professional wrestling. Her accomplishments opened doors for other women to pursue careers outside of professional wrestling.

6. Media Attention and Mainstream Recognition: Due to Sytch's fame, the wrestling world as a whole paid attention to him in the media. During a time of growing cultural prominence, her appearances in magazines, interviews, and public appearances helped to establish professional wrestling's wider popularity.

Tammy Sytch's ascent to fame was evidence of her diverse skill set, which combined business savvy with an enticing demeanor. She became a pioneer for women in professional wrestling at this time in her career and had a lasting impression on the business. But as her career took off, she faced personal setbacks that changed the story of her in the years that followed.

CHAPTER 2: REVEALED OF PERSONAL ISSUES

Along with the rise to fame that characterized Tammy Sytch's career in professional wrestling, her troubles on a personal level slowly surfaced. Her story became more complicated as a result of her challenges, both inside and beyond the wrestling arena.

1. drug misuse Challenges: As Sytch managed the rigors of her emerging profession, allegations of drug misuse started to appear. Her struggle with addiction became a visible part of her life, affecting her well-being and causing several difficulties.

2. Unstable connections: One of Sytch's main areas of trouble was his connections. These turbulent and turbulent relationships often transpired in public, which increased the level of scrutiny and criticism around her personal life.

3. Legal Difficulties: In addition to her difficulties, Sytch had legal issues. Legal entanglements clouded her once-glistening career, ranging from drug misuse concerns to various legal complications.

4. Effect on Professional Status: Sytch's professional status started to suffer as a result of her issues. Despite her past achievements, the wrestling community saw a decrease in her prominence in the business, illustrating the interdependence of the personal and professional domains.

5. Repercussions in the Public Eye: The media and general public became aware of Sytch's troubles as they developed. Tabloids and wrestling magazines began to follow her trip, reporting on the difficulties she encountered outside the ring.

6. Rehabilitation endeavors: Sytch made public rehabilitation endeavors despite the difficulties. Among these attempts were resolving her concerns that had turned into public spectacles and getting assistance for her drug addiction problems. However, there were many obstacles in the way of rehabilitation.

7. Constant Struggle Cycle: The disclosure of Sytch's hardships revealed a continuous cycle entwined with her career story. Her off-screen struggles became intrinsic to her wrestling heritage, adding to a convoluted and often tragic plot.

Once hidden behind the glamor of the wrestling platform, Tammy Sytch's battles emerged as a moving and widely discussed facet of her life, highlighting the fine line that exists between the human costs of fame and celebrity. As her tale developed, it brought up issues of the industry's duty to its performers as well as the influence of personal hardships on a wrestler's career.

2:1 DIFFICULTIES OUTSIDE OF THE RINGS

Obstacles Beyond the Rings: Exposing Tammy Sytch's Individual Battles

Outside of the clamor of the fans and the spectacle of the wrestling arena, Tammy Sytch, also known as Sunny, had to overcome several very difficult obstacles in her private life. The story outside the rings showed a multifaceted mosaic of hardships:

1. The battles Tammy Sytch had with drug misuse became well-known aspects of her life. Fans of professional wrestling and the media saw her struggle with addiction, bringing attention to the negative effects it had on her career and general well-being.

2. Rocky connections in the Spotlight: Sytch's private life was under more scrutiny as personal connections were shown on a public platform. Complicating her issues outside of the arena of wrestling were turbulent relationships, which became a topic of conversation.

3. Legal Difficulties and Judicial Proceedings: Legal issues were apparent as a major obstacle for Sytch. Her judicial struggles were entwined with the story of her life outside of the ring, ranging from accusations of drug addiction to various legal difficulties.

4. A Professional Reduction During a Personal Crisis:

The personal challenges that Sytch encountered outside of the ring started to cloud her once bright professional future. Her reputation within the profession suffered as a result of Wrestling promoters' struggles with personal concerns.

5. Public Scrutiny and Media Attention: The public and media kept a close eye on Sytch's struggles as they developed. Tabloids and wrestling magazines chronicled the highs and lows of her career, bringing her life under severe public scrutiny.

6. Efforts at Redemption and Rehabilitation: Despite the hardships, Sytch made efforts at redemption in public. The story continued to take on new dimensions as a result of her attempts to deal with her drug misuse problems and save her personal and professional lives.

7. Effect on Legacy and Wrestling Community: **Outside** of the ring, Sytch faced hardships that resonated with the wrestling community and left an enduring effect on his legacy. Her experience made people consider the industry's support networks as well as the toll that stardom and personal hardships may have on its artists.

"Challenges Outside the Rings" captures Tammy Sytch's turbulent path and illuminates the human side of a wrestling celebrity battling personal issues in a world where attention is never off the spotlight.

2:2 INFLUENCE ON TAMMY SYTCH'S PRIVATE LIFE: AN UNCOVERED JOURNEY

The difficulties that Tammy Sytch faced outside of the wrestling ring weighed heavily on her personal life and had a lasting effect on her journey:

1. Substance misuse Struggles: Substance misuse had a significant negative influence on Sytch's personal life. In addition to impairing her physical health, addiction damaged her relationships, undermined her trust, and created a vicious cycle of inner agony.

2. Connection Unrest in Public View: Highly publicized partnerships introduced a further level of difficulty. The world saw Sytch's emotional troubles as a result of the public scrutiny around her love relationships, which shaped opinions and added to the story of her turbulent personal life.

Legal entanglements had a detrimental effect on Sytch's personal life, exposing her to several court fights and judicial challenges. The legal battles affected not only her independence but also her general well-being and day-to-day life in significant ways.

3. Decline in Profession A direct effect on Sytch's sense of identity was the fall in her professional status as a result of personal issues. She had come to depend heavily on wrestling, and her general well-being suffered as a result of that relationship eroding.

4. Efforts at Rehabilitation: Sytch's path toward recovery demonstrated a resolute attempt to take back command of her own life. Although a start in the right direction, the effect of rehabilitation efforts also highlighted the continuous fight to overcome deeply ingrained obstacles.

5. Public Scrutiny and Emotional Cost: Sytch suffered an emotional cost as a result of constant public scrutiny. She had more strain and emotional complexity in her daily life as a result of the media's frequent exposure to her issues.

6. Legacy and Interactions within the Wrestling Community: The influence went beyond interpersonal interactions to include the larger wrestling community. Sytch's struggles affected the others she met in the business, changing people's opinions and posing more general questions about the systems in place to assist artists going through difficult times.

"Impact on Tammy Sytch's Personal Life"
explores the emotional and relational aspects of a
journey that transpired both within and outside of
the limelight of professional wrestling, delving into
the complex interaction between personal issues
and the individual.

CHAPTER 3: DECLINE IN CAREER

Tammy Sytch's decline from wrestling stardom throughout her career

Former professional wrestler Tammy Sytch went through a serious career slump that was characterized by several difficulties and setbacks:

1. Change in the Path of Wrestling:
  Tammy Sytch's wrestling career took an unexpected turn as the late 1990s went on. Her status in the main wrestling organizations declined as a result of personal issues and changes in the profession.

2. Professional obstacles and Changing Roles:
Sytch had obstacles in his career, which included leaving prominent managing positions. Her position

changed as a result of the shifting dynamics inside wrestling organizations, which lessened the effect she formerly had as the main character in stories.

3. Effect of Personal challenges: Substance misuse and legal troubles were two major personal challenges that contributed to Sytch's decline in his job. Her professional reputation suffered as a result of the well-publicized difficulties she had outside of the ring, which affected her dependability and marketability.

4. Diminished Visibility in Mainstream Wrestling: Sytch's prominence in mainstream wrestling organizations decreased as his struggles worsened. Aware of the possible dangers linked to her problems, the industry was more reluctant to include her heavily in plots and events.

5. Lessened Wrestling Legacy: One factor that led to a lessened wrestling legacy was Sytch's career collapse. Previously praised for her management abilities and on-screen persona, her disappearance from the limelight was a significant shift from her prior achievements.

6. Difficulties Getting possibilities: Sytch found it harder and harder to get fresh possibilities in the wrestling business. Her issues gained a connotation that hindered her from getting jobs and regaining the momentum she had previously had.

7. Effect on Professional Relationships: Within the wrestling world, Sytch's career decline had an impact on professional relationships. Her obstacles affected her reputation among spectators, other wrestlers, and promoters, which in turn affected her possibilities.

8. Tense Relationship with the crowd: Sytch struggled to keep up a favorable public image, which was seen in the tense relationship he had with the wrestling crowd, who had earlier been ardent in their advocacy. This signified a big change in her connection with wrestling fans compared to her former status as a fan favorite.

The book **"Career Downturn: Tammy Sytch's Descent from Wrestling Stardom"** effectively conveys the intricacies and obstacles that resulted in a shift in Sytch's career trajectory. This stage of her career captures the complex relationship between her challenges and the harsh realities of the professional wrestling world.

3:1 CHANGE IN WRESTLING TRAJECTORIES

Shift in Wrestling Trajectories: Tammy Sytch's Progress in the Field

Tammy Sytch's professional wrestling career saw a significant turning point when she entered the complex realm of professional wrestling.

1. Early Ascent in Smoky Mountain Wrestling (SMW): Sytch showed potential in her early career as a wrestler in Smoky Mountain Wrestling. Her lively personality attracted the attention of industry insiders as well as fans, and her work as a valet and manager laid the scene for future accomplishments.

2. Transfer to World Wrestling Federation (WWF): Sytch's move to the World Wrestling Federation (WWF) marked a turning point. She advanced significantly in her wrestling career when she signed with one of the top organizations in the business, which gave her a bigger stage on which to display her managing abilities.

3. Managerial Talent and Title Achievement: Throughout the WWF, Sytch's talent as a manager increased, leading groups like The Bodydonnas to titles. She cemented her place as an important figure in the wrestling industry with her ability to improve storylines and boost the performance of the stars under her management.

4. Creative Storylines and Promotional Effects: Sytch's participation in creative storylines marked a turning point in her wrestling career. Her on-screen persona and participation in promotional events enhanced the entertainment value of wrestling, influencing not only specific bouts but also the storyline of the business overall.

5. Challenges and the Emergence of Personal Struggles: Substance misuse and legal troubles were among the personal struggles that caused an unanticipated turn in the trajectory. These difficulties started to have an impact on Sytch's personal and professional lives, which caused a dramatic change in the story of her career.

6. Diminished Role in Promotions: As a result of the changing landscape, major wrestling promotions saw a decline in their influence. Once on an upward track, Sytch's career in wrestling suffered a downturn in prospects as her issues and the realities of the profession came together.

The alteration in Sytch's wrestling career path had an immediate effect on character dynamics. The previously colorful and prominent character now had to navigate new terrain, with her portrayal in the wrestling plots shifting as her troubles became more and more of a plotline.

8. Attempts at Atonement and Future Prospects: Sytch started making efforts at Atonement when the wrestling career took a different turn. Her attempts to overcome personal obstacles and her road toward recovery marked a new chapter in her wrestling career, one that might potentially affect how she develops going forward.

"Wrestling Trajectory Shift: Tammy Sytch's Evolution in the Industry" captures the complex life of a wrestling celebrity whose trajectory—which was originally characterized by ascent—saw a radical change brought about by factors related to both her personal and professional life.

3:2 WORKPLACE FAILURES

Professional Mistakes: Tammy Sytch's Difficulties in the Ring

In the realm of professional wrestling, Tammy Sytch, sometimes known as Sunny, suffered a string of unfortunate events that clouded her once-vibrant career. These losses, which were indicative of the difficulties encountered both within and outside the ring, signaled a turning point in Sytch's journey:

1. managing Role Changes: When Sytch made changes to its managing duties, the first indications of a professional setback appeared. Her on-screen duties changed as a result of the dynamics of wrestling companies and artistic choices, which changed her influence on plots and wrestling narratives.

2. shift from the spotlight: Sytch went through a shift from the spotlight as the wrestling scene changed. Her character's exposure decreased as a result of shifting dynamics in the business, which affected her capacity to engage the audience deeply.

3. Struggles Despite Championship Success: Sytch had personal challenges, such as drug misuse and legal troubles, at the same time as his professional losses, despite prior championship victories. These difficulties affected her dependability and capacity to keep her word and also had an impact on her wrestling career.

4. Diminished Opportunities and Trust: Sytch's professional losses caused promoters and wrestling companies to lose faith in him. She received fewer parts and appearances as a result of the industry's understanding of her struggles, thus impacting the chances available to her.

5. Effect on Storyline Dynamics: The way that stories wrestled with the changing problems had an effect. Formerly a pivotal role in generating stories, Sytch discovered that her challenges affected the way others saw her, resulting in changed interactions between characters.

6. Industry reluctance and Caution: The wrestling industry had some reluctance as a result of the professional defeats. Promoters and groups cautiously approached Sytch, restricting her participation in high-profile narratives and events, aware of the difficulties she faced.

7. Public Perception and Image Effects: Sytch's professional disappointments had an impact on how the public saw him. The audience's perception of the once-admired wrestling star changed as a result of the difficulties she suffered both inside and outside the ring.

8. Strained Relationships within the Wrestling Community: The wrestling community had strained relationships as a result of the professional defeats. Promoters, fans, and colleagues all saw a change in Sytch's reputation, which led to a complex and sometimes tense relationship with those who had previously been a part of her wrestling career.

The book **"Professional Setbacks**: Tammy Sytch's Challenges in the Wrestling Arena" explores the complex relationship between a person's issues and how those struggles affect their wrestling profession. This chapter of Sytch's story sheds light on the nuances of the field and the fine line that separates professional achievement from the obstacles that lie outside of the public eye.

CHAPTER 4: UNREST IN THE LAW

Legal Unrest: Tammy Sytch's Journey Beyond the Ring in Law

Tammy Sytch's personal and professional path got even more convoluted when her wrestling career became caught in a web of legal trouble. The legal difficulties she encountered were an important element in her life story:

1. Substance-Related Legal Troubles:
Substance-related troubles played a significant role in Sytch's legal tumult. Substance abuse-related arrests and court cases emerged as a recurrent motif, emphasizing how personal hardships affected her legal status.

2. Several Arrests and Custodial Stays:
Throughout the legal ordeal, Sytch was the subject of several arrests, each of which signaled a well-known incident in his life. She started to have custodial stints, and every arrest made her problems more severe, both within and outside of the wrestling community.

3. Issues with Probation and Violations: Sytch had difficulties with probation, a legal matter that kept coming up in her court cases. She became even more entangled in the judicial system as a result of probation term violations.

4. Court Appearances and Legal Processes: As the legal processes developed, Sytch's court appearances became a regular feature of her life. Her challenges gained further public attention as a result of the public's scrutiny of every development and the media coverage of the court cases.

5. Effect on Personal Finances: Sytch's finances suffered as a result of the legal unrest. Legal bills, penalties, and possible payouts added to her already heavy load, impacting her financial security and making an already difficult time even more stressful.

6. Strained connections with the Legal System: Sytch's connections with the legal system were strained as the number of legal challenges increased. Frequent interactions with members of the judicial and law enforcement community began to symbolize a never-ending cycle that reflected the intricate relationship between legal ramifications and human issues.

7. Media Attention and Public Scrutiny: Sytch's legal tumult drew significant media coverage and public scrutiny. Every legal incident made headlines, influencing public opinion and adding to the story of her life outside of the ring.

**8. Efforts at Legal Redemption and
Rehabilitation:** In the face of legal disputes, Sytch
made open efforts at rehabilitation. Her path gained
complexity from the legal redemption story, which
illustrated the continuous battle to balance personal
demons with the requirements of the judicial
system.

"Legal Turmoil: Tammy Sytch's Legal Odyssey
Beyond the Ring" delves into the complex
relationship that shaped a pivotal period in Sytch's
life between her troubles and the legal
ramifications. With the judicial unrest providing a
background for the larger story, it highlights the
difficulties that prominent figures have navigating
the court system.

4:1 NEW LEGAL CONCERNS: TAMMY SYTCH'S DISSECTING LEGAL ENVIRONMENT

Tammy Sytch, better known as Sunny in the wrestling community, became entangled in a complex web of legal troubles that complicated her story on both the personal and professional fronts:

1. Substance Addiction-Related Charges: Substance addiction was a significant factor in the emergence of legal difficulties for Sytch. Her tale had recurrent legal themes stemming from charges of possession of controlled drugs and driving while intoxicated.

2. Several Arrests and Booking Episodes: Several arrests and booking episodes were the result of emerging legal concerns. Every arrest turned into a well-reported incident, a publicized phase in Sytch's legal ordeal.

3. Probation Violations and Legal Repercussions: Sytch encountered probation violations as legal difficulties grew. These infractions resulted in legal ramifications, which made her continuous battles more complicated and exacerbated the legal maze.

4. Court Appearances and Legal Proceedings: As the legal difficulties concerning Sytch emerged, courtrooms became a regular background. The media meticulously followed her legal trip, which was characterized by hearings and appearances, as the processes played out like a public drama.

5. Financial Strain and Legal Costs: Sytch's financial stability suffered as a result of the arising legal concerns. Financial strains from legal fees, penalties, and possible settlements added to her total financial difficulties.

6. Public Scrutiny and Media Spotlight: The public became aware of Sytch's legal disputes. Media sources kept a close eye on the developing legal drama, developing a storyline that transcended the wrestling ring and became a center of interest in the larger entertainment world.

The emergence of legal troubles had an impact on Sytch's career chances in the wrestling business. Promoters and groups handled their engagements cautiously out of concern over possible legal issues, which affected her ability to get parts and appearances.

8. Efforts at Legal Redemption: Sytch made open efforts at legal redemption in the face of mounting legal difficulties. Rehabilitating herself and dealing with legal matters became part of her story as she worked to get over the legal obstacles that characterized this stage of her life.

"**Emerging Legal Issues:** Tammy Sytch's Unraveling Legal Landscape" depicts the courtroom drama that developed into a pivotal part of Sytch's path. This period of her life highlights the intricate relationship that exists between her challenges, the legal ramifications, and the public perception, creating a story that goes much beyond the professional wrestling arena.

4:2 DISSECTING THE IMAGE

Tammy Sytch's Journey Beyond Wrestling Stardom: Dissecting a Reputation

Tammy Sytch, who was once known as Sunny in the professional wrestling industry, saw a significant decline in her reputation—a trip complicated by issues that did not just arise within the wrestling ring:

1. Becoming a Wrestling Icon: In the 1990s, Sytch became a well-known and prominent wrestler after rising to prominence. She became a legend in the wrestling industry because of her management responsibilities and on-screen persona.

2. Changes in Career Trajectories: Changes in Sytch's career trajectory marked the beginning of the unraveling of her reputation. Shifts in the wrestling scene and personal challenges changed the story and clouded her once-brilliant image.

3. Legal Unrest and Public Inquisitiveness: Legal matters, such as many apprehensions and courtroom scenes, emerged as major themes in the disintegration of Sytch's image. As each legal incident unfolded in the media, public scrutiny grew, casting doubt on the favorable reputation she had established throughout her wrestling career.

4. Personal Challenges and Public Exposure: Sytch's public persona became entwined with personal challenges, namely related to drug usage. The public's observation of her struggles caused her reputation to disintegrate, making it more difficult to distinguish between the real person behind the scenes and the wrestler.

The deteriorating reputation of Sytch had an immediate effect on his professional status. Her once-high profile began to erode as wrestling promoters, cautious about the possible dangers linked to her struggles, stopped featuring her regularly.

6. Financial Stress and Legal Repercussions:
The financial stress brought on by the legal repercussions added yet another level to the reputation's disintegrating facade. In addition to financial strains on her, fines, court fees, and possible settlements also hurt her reputation.

7. Attempts at atonement Despite Difficulties:
Sytch made discernible efforts at atonement despite the difficulties. Taking part in public rehabilitation programs and dealing with personal matters became part of her quest to preserve what little of her image remained.

8. Strained Relationships and Public Opinion:
The wrestling community's relationships were strained as a result of the unraveling reputation, and public opinion was changed. Once respected for her contributions to the field, Sytch discovered that her hardships eclipsed her prior successes in the field.

"Unraveling of a Reputation: Tammy Sytch's Journey Beyond Wrestling Stardom" is the complex and multidimensional tale of a wrestler whose reputation saw a significant shift. This period in Sytch's life illustrates the complex interactions between legal issues, personal struggles, and the harshness of public opinion.

CHAPTER 5: THE CRITICAL JUNCTURE

The Decisive Event: Tammy Sytch's Intersection with Wrestling and Life

As Sunny, Tammy Sytch—who has become a household name in the wrestling world—met a turning point that would alter both her professional and personal lives:

1. Ascendance to Wrestling prominence: Sytch's ascent to wrestling prominence in the 1990s marked the beginning of the path leading up to the crucial moment. She shot to fame thanks to her personality, management skills, and on-screen allure, becoming a significant player in the wrestling world.

2. Changes in the Professional environment:
The turning point occurred when changes in the
professional environment changed the path that
Sytch had blazed. The industry's changing
dynamics along with changes inside wrestling
companies prepared her for a major career turning
point.

3. Emergence of Personal difficulties: The
emergence of personal difficulties coincided with
the key period. Problems with drug misuse and
legal entanglements started to show, shrouding
Sytch's once-dazzling wrestling character and
marking a watershed in her life.

4. Legal Unrest and Public Examining: A critical
turning point during the decisive period was the
legal unrest. After many arrests and court cases,
Sytch became well-known, drawing intense
attention and shattering the carefully constructed
persona she had worked so hard to cultivate during
her career as a wrestler.

5. Effect on Professional Status: Sytch's professional status was significantly impacted by the critical event. Aware of the possible dangers linked to her struggles, wrestling promoters adjusted their interactions with her, which resulted in a drop in opportunities and a reassessment of her place in the business.

6. Financial Stress and Legal Repercussions: One important element of the turning point was the financial stress brought on by the legal repercussions. Sytch's path became even more complicated due to fines, legal fees, and the wider economic effects of court cases.

7. Efforts at Rehabilitation and Redemption: At this critical juncture, Sytch made his public efforts at rehabilitation. In an attempt to get over the obstacles that marked this significant turning point in her life, she focused on her rehabilitation and dealt with personal issues.

8. Effect on Personal Identity: The turning point compelled an examination of one's own identity. As the reality of her troubles clashed with the wrestling character she had developed, Sytch struggled not just with the obstacles in her career but also with the severe influence on her sense of self.

The book **"The Pivotal Moment:** Tammy Sytch's Crossroads in Wrestling and Life" chronicles a pivotal time in the life of a legendary wrestler. This story examines the complex interactions that occurred between personal struggles, career achievement, and the crucial choices made at a turning point with potentially significant consequences.

5:1 IMPORTANT OCCURRENCES THAT CAUSE CHANGE

Crucial Moments That Caused Change: Tammy Sytch's Revolutionary Path

The following significant incidents caused Tammy Sytch's life to drastically alter, both within and outside of the wrestling industry:

1. Wrestling Prominence and Early Success: The story starts with Sytch's rise to wrestling prominence, where her talent as a manager and her alluring on-screen persona won her a lot of praise. Early triumph prepared the way for a voyage that would shortly be characterized by pivotal events.

2. Changes in Wrestling Dynamics: Important things happened when the dynamics of the wrestling business changed, changing Sytch's status and function. Alterations in the promotions and creative paths hinted at a coming metamorphosis that threatened the security of her well-established character as a wrestler.

3. Emergence of Personal troubles: The disclosure of Sytch's troubles to the public was the first significant occurrence. Her history of substance misuse and legal troubles surfaced, interrupting a vulnerable moment and paving the way for a personal and professional life assessment.

4. Legal Unrest and Public Examining Eyes: Unrest in the legal system emerged as a focal point and constituted an important event that transpired under the harsh scrutiny of the public. The difficulties became more intense as a result of many arrests and court cases, which brought Sytch to the public's notice and drastically changed opinions about her wrestling career.

5. Effect on Career Opportunities: The important incidents changed the professional environment in

Sytch. Wrestling promoters, aware of the dangers linked to her struggles, adjusted their interactions, which affected her chances and worsened her reputation in the business.

6. Financial hardship and Legal Consequences: Sytch's trip grew more complicated due to the financial hardship brought on by legal repercussions. Legal fees, fines, and the wider financial effects of court cases highlighted the significant life changes she was experiencing.

7. Efforts at Rehabilitation and Redemption: When Sytch made his first public efforts at rehabilitation, a crucial turning point occurred. Participating in rehabilitation programs turned into a proactive move to deal with personal issues and reconstruct a life that had gotten enmeshed in legal issues.

8. Identity Reckoning and Inner Growth: Sytch had to face the collision between her wrestling character and the reality of her inner troubles as a result of the pivotal occurrences. This period of reflection served as a springboard for resilience, personal development, and the quest for a revitalized sense of self.

The book "Critical Events Leading to Change: Tammy Sytch's Transformative Journey" summarizes the set of critical events that marked a significant turning point in Sytch's life. This story delves into the complex interactions between her emotional struggles, legal obstacles, and the pivotal choices that eventually formed the next phase of her journey.

5:2 IMPORTANT MILESTONES IN SYTCH'S LIFE

Significant Events in Tammy Sytch's Life: Handling the Challenging Path

Tammy Sytch's life story is replete with dramatic moments that signal critical turning points in the development of her narratives, both personally and professionally:

1. Ascend to Wrestling Stardom: In the 1990s, Sytch made his way to the top of the wrestling world. Her captivating demeanor and adept administrative skills catapulted her into the spotlight, paving the way for a career that would soon encounter revolutionary obstacles.

2. Changes in Wrestling Dynamics: Sytch's role underwent a transformation that marked turning moments in the story. It was necessary to reassess her status and influence in the wrestling community because of changes in the business that indicated a shift from her previous prominent role.

3. Revealing Personal troubles: The disclosure of Sytch's troubles to the public marked a significant turning point. The public's discovery of substance usage problems and legal complications exposed weaknesses and sparked a moment of introspection.

4. Legal unrest and Public Dissection: The pivotal moments became more intense as legal unrest exposed Sytch to the intense light of public scrutiny. Numerous arrests and court cases turned out to be pivotal events that drastically changed people's opinions of the wrestling legend and added intricacies to her career.

5. Effect on Professional Status: Significant events had an impact on Sytch's professional status in the wrestling business. Aware of the dangers connected to her struggles, wrestling promoters adjusted their engagements, which resulted in a drop in opportunities and a reassessment of her position.

6. Financial hardship and legal repercussions: The burden on finances brought on by legal repercussions constituted a crucial turning point. Fines, court fees, and financial ramifications highlighted the significant life changes for Sytch and added another level of complication to her already complicated personal and financial situation.

7. Efforts to Redeem and Rehabilitate:

As Sytch started making public efforts at atonement, a pivotal moment occurred. Participating in rehabilitation activities turned into an active step in tackling personal issues, signifying a will to go over the obstacles that characterized this stage of her life.

8. Identity Reckoning and Personal Growth:

Sytch had an identity reckoning as a result of the turning moments, which forced her to face the conflict between her wrestling character and her true challenges. This period of reflection served as a springboard for resilience, personal development, and the quest for a revitalized sense of self.

Tammy Sytch's life story, "Turning Points in Tammy Sytch's Life: Navigating the Tumultuous Journey," captures the critical events that have woven the complex fabric of Sytch's life. This story examines the transformational potential of choices and circumstances, shedding light on the complicated interactions between legal issues, personal hardships, and the quest for forgiveness in the face of misfortune.

CHAPTER 6: LIFE IN PRISON

Tammy Sytch's Incarceration and the Battle for Redemption: Life Behind Bars

Once a shining star in the professional wrestling industry, Tammy Sytch now had to navigate the harsh realities of life in prison. This was a struggle, an opportunity for reflection, and a never-ending search for atonement.

1. Legal Unrest Concluding in Sytch's Incarceration: The story took a significant turn when legal unrest led to Sytch's imprisonment. Her previous dazzling existence in the limelight of professional wrestling was drastically different from her spell of incarceration after many arrests and court disputes.

2. Facing the Hard Reality of Incarceration:
Living in prison made Sytch face the harsh reality of solitary confinement. She faced challenges to her perseverance and mental fortitude daily, including the loss of personal independence, monotonous regimentation, and isolation from the outside world.

3. Issues Regarding Substance Abuse Behind Prison Walls: Substance abuse issues continue to exist behind prison walls. Sytch's battles with addiction persisted, demonstrating the ubiquity of inner monsters that escaped the concrete confines of prison.

4. Attempts at Personal Development and Rehabilitation: Sytch's life in prison served as a harsh testing ground for his attempts at recovery. She looked for opportunities for personal development and atonement via self-reflection, therapy, and prison programs. She was eager to leave jail.

5. Handling Interactions in a Carceral Setting: In a correctional setting, the dynamics of interpersonal interactions experienced a distinct metamorphosis. Sytch offered a window into the microcosm of interpersonal relationships behind prison walls by navigating the difficulties of friendships and contacts with other prisoners.

6. Effect on Well-Being and Mental Health:

Sytch's general well-being and mental health suffered greatly as a result of being behind bars. Prison's isolation, difficulties, and uncertainty turned into strong roadblocks that shaped her coping skills and emotional fortitude.

7. Legal Conflicts and Possible Routes to Freedom: Sytch's existence in prison was not exempt from legal conflicts. As she worked her way through the maze of legal options that may set her free, appeals, parole issues, and the possibility of legal redemption were critical components.

8. The Story Continued to Pursue Atonement After Release: Sytch's quest for atonement continued beyond the prison gates. Life after release turned into a crucial phase that brought attention to the continuous difficulties in reintegrating into both the wrestling community and society at large.

"Life Behind Bars: Tammy Sytch's Incarceration and the Struggle for Redemption" sheds light on the life-changing experience of a prominent wrestler who must deal with the fallout from her deeds. This story examines the difficulties of living behind bars and the never-ending search for atonement against the background of court cases, individual hardships, and the hope for a better life outside of jail.

Detention: Tammy Sytch's Seclusion and Individual Journey

When Tammy Sytch faced a term of jail, her life took a drastically different turn. This new chapter had its own set of complications, difficulties, and chances for introspection.

1. Legal Unrest That Led to Imprisonment:

Tammy Sytch's imprisonment was the result of legal unrest that started the path toward incarceration. After many court cases, legal disputes, and arrests, a judge decided to put her behind bars.

2. Life Beneath the Constraints of Confinement:

Daily regimentation and routines behind prison walls are a consequence of incarceration. The regimented setting, less autonomy, and limited social connections became distinguishing characteristics of Sytch's day-to-day life.

3. Problems with Substance Misuse in Prison:
Substance misuse remained a problem even behind prison walls. As someone who had to navigate addiction in a controlled setting, Sytch demonstrated the persistent persistence of inner challenges regardless of external conditions.

4. Efforts at Rehabilitation Behind Bars: Despite the constraints, Sytch participated in several rehabilitation initiatives while incarcerated. She welcomed chances for personal development and looked for ways to address the underlying problems that resulted in her imprisonment, from therapy to educational programs.

5. Handling Relationships in a Carceral Environment: In a correctional setting, relationships experience a special kind of change. Through navigating the nuances of interpersonal relationships with other prisoners, Sytch provided insight into the complicated network of alliances and obstacles that characterize life behind bars.

6. Effects on Emotional and Mental Health:
One tragic part of Sytch's imprisonment was the toll it had on her emotional and mental health. Prison life's isolation, uncertainty, and constraints shaped her fortitude, emphasizing the environment's deep psychological effect.

7. Legal challenges and the Pursuit of Freedom:
Throughout Sytch's imprisonment, legal challenges remained a part of her story. Appeals, parole considerations, and the legal routes leading to possible release were essential elements in her judicial navigation from behind prison walls.

8. Continued Journey Beyond Release: The story explores the difficulties of reintegrating into society after the term of imprisonment. Following his release from jail, Sytch's journey became a pivotal chapter characterized by the difficult task of reconstructing his life outside of prison and his constant search for atonement.

Confinement and Personal Odyssey by Tammy Sytch illuminates the complex aspects of life behind bars. Although it was a time of limitations and difficulties, it also offered chances for self-reflection, rehabilitation, and the quest for a new identity while confined to the prison system.

6:2 REALITIES:

Tammy Sytch's Unfiltered Path Through Truths and Difficulties

The life of Tammy Sytch is a tapestry of harsh realities, where every thread reveals the raw core of her path through hardships and truths:

1. dazzling Realities and Wrestling Stardom:
The adventure began with the dazzling realities of
professional wrestling. Sytch created a glossy
façade with his charm and management skills,
paving the way for a career that shone in the
limelight of praise and success.

2. Changes in Professional Realities: As the
wrestling world evolved, so did the realities. The
wrestling world was changing, and Sytch had to
reevaluate the reality she faced as a result of
changes inside the business that changed her
career path.

3. Revealing Personal problems: The
unvarnished voyage revealed the brutal truths of
individual problems. The emergence of substance
misuse problems and legal complications exposed
the weaknesses that went beyond the wrestling
character and demonstrated the connection
between personal and professional reality.

4. Realities of Legal Unrest and Public Scrutiny: As legal unrest grew, Sytch became more visible to the public. Numerous arrests and court cases turned into stark chapters that exposed the unvarnished truth of the difficulties she encountered in the harsh light of public and media scrutiny.

5. Impact on Professional Realities: There was a significant change in the realities of professional status. Aware of the dangers that come with personal struggles, wrestling promoters adjusted the terms of their agreements, which resulted in a drop in opportunities and a reassessment of Sytch's place in the business.

6. Economic Stress and Legal Repercussions Realities: The burden on finances brought on by potential legal repercussions created an additional level of difficulty. Penalties, court expenses, and financial ramifications highlighted the significant life transformations in Sytch, exposing raw facts that extended beyond the professional wrestling arena.

7. Attempts at Redemption and Rehabilitation

Realities: Sytch's open attempts at redemption were part of the uncensored path. By participating in rehabilitation programs, she was able to demonstrate her dedication to conquering obstacles in her life and expose the unvarnished truths of a transforming endeavor.

8. Identity Reckoning and Personal Growth

Realities: Amidst personal challenges, Sytch had to face certain realities about who she was. Her period of introspection turned into a testing ground for her perseverance, personal development, and the quest for a fresh sense of self—an unvarnished examination of her humanity.

Realities: The unadulterated realities of a wrestling personality's life are captured in Tammy Sytch's Unfiltered Journey Amidst Truths and Trials. This story examines the dynamics between triumph and failure, public praise and criticism, and the unwavering quest for atonement among the raw facts that make up Tammy Sytch's singular path.

6:3 GETTING BY WHILE CONFINED

Resilience in the Face of Imprisonment: Tammy Sytch's Story

Throughout her time behind bars, Tammy Sytch showed a strong will to overcome obstacles and show off her diverse array of coping strategies, development, and quest for atonement.

1. Adjusting to the Strict Rituals of Prison Life: Sytch began adjusting to the strict rituals of prison life to cope with his incarceration. With its rigid rules and timetables, the controlled environment served as the background against which she started to develop her resistance.

2. Facing Personal Challenges in the Confines:
Sytch's road toward coping became tragic as he faced personal challenges within the prison walls. The obstacles of drug misuse and the intricacies of inner demons continued, necessitating a high degree of fortitude in the confined space.

3. Participating in Rehabilitation Programs:
Sytch's coping mechanisms took a proactive turn when he participated in several prison system rehabilitation programs. Therapy sessions, educational programs, and counseling turned into opportunities for her to better herself and deal with the underlying problems that led to her imprisonment.

4. Handling Interactions in a Carceral Context:
Coping was extended to the dynamics of interactions in the prison setting. By navigating the complexities of establishing relationships with other prisoners, Sytch offered an insight into the

microcosm of human interactions that shaped her social environment behind bars.

5. Effect on Mental Health and Emotional Resilience: One of the most important aspects of Sytch's path was learning to cope with the toll on her mental health. She had to develop adaptive coping methods to withstand the psychological pressure of living in jail because of the emotional obstacles, loneliness, and uncertainty that come with it.

6. Fighting for Freedom and Using Coping Mechanisms: Sytch used coping mechanisms in conjunction with fighting for freedom. Appeals, parole considerations, and negotiating the convoluted legal system while confined were essential parts of her coping strategies.

7. Sustaining a Quest for Personal Development: As Sytch looked for ways to better himself within the confines of jail life, coping turned into a quest for personal development. Accepting learning chances and developing her skills turned into essential elements of her coping mechanisms and resilience.

8. Persistent Pursuit of Redemption beyond Bars: Sytch's post-release path emerged as a pivotal chapter, demonstrating how coping with incarceration stretched beyond the prison walls. Her ongoing quest for atonement and a changed life outside of prison was based on the strength she developed while inside.

Tammy Sytch's book, Coping with Confinement: Resilience Behind Bars, sheds light on the many techniques a wrestling celebrity uses to deal with the difficulties of prison. This story delves into the intricacies of managing oneself, individual growth, and the resilient spirit that drove Tammy Sytch beyond the hardships of imprisonment and into the hope of a revitalized future.

CHAPTER 7: CONTEMPLATING A LOST HERITAGE

Thinking Back on a Lost Heritage: Tammy Sytch's Wrestling Adventure

Once a brilliant trip through the glamor and flash of fame, Tammy Sytch's wrestling career turned into a story of introspection on a legacy tarnished by personal hardships, legal issues, and the unstoppable march of time:

1. The story starts in the heyday of professional wrestling in the 1990s, when Tammy Sytch, popularly known as Sunny, became a powerful manager and a captivating character. At first, her legacy was brilliant and added to the golden era of wrestling.

2. **Shifts in the Landscape:** The wrestling landscape is changing while the contemplation takes place. A transformational time was characterized by shifts in creative orientations, promotions, and the changing dynamics of the wrestling business, which put doubt on Sytch's formerly exalted standing within the wrestling world.

3. **Unveiling Personal issues:** When personal issues emerge, the story explores how the legacy is falling apart. Problems with substance addiction and legal entanglements developed into moving chapters that exposed the frailties that undermined the once-vibrant aura of Tammy Sytch's wrestling heritage.

4. **Legal Unrest and Public Scrutiny:** As Sytch deals with repeated arrests and court cases while facing intense public scrutiny, the contemplation becomes more profound amid legal unrest. Courtroom dramas and the legacy of wrestling

combine to create a complicated story with several levels of depth.

5. Effect on Professional Position: The effect on Sytch's professional position in the wrestling business highlights the fading legacy. Promotions reevaluate their engagements due to a decrease in opportunities and a reassessment of their job because they are wary of the dangers that come with personal issues.

6. Economic Stress and Legal Repercussions: The contemplation encompasses the economic stress arising from legal ramifications. In the larger scheme of the wrestling community, fines, legal fees, and financial ramifications become harsh realities that further erode Sytch's legacy.

7. Attempts at Redemption and Recovery: Sytch's contemplation includes public attempts at recovery, which gives the story a redeeming tone. A crucial part of the trip is her involvement in recovery programs, which she uses to clarify and recover her legacy from the shadow of her troubles.

8. Legacy Enduring Wrestling: The contemplation encompasses the legacy that exists outside of the squared circle and goes beyond the boundaries of wrestling. Sytch's journey through wrestling becomes a symbol of perseverance, development, and the never-ending quest for atonement—a legacy that goes beyond victories and defeats.

Thinking Back on a Lost Legacy: Tammy Sytch's Wrestling Odyssey depicts the intricate path of a legendary wrestler navigating both personal and professional obstacles. This story examines the reflective times, court cases, and the unwavering spirit of atonement that mold the contemplation on a heritage that, despite its flaws, continues to be a crucial component of the wrestling story.

Diminished Wrestling Legacy: Tammy Sytch's Journey Through Shadows

Tammy Sytch's once-illustrious wrestling reputation suffered a significant decline, with her path clouded by personal hardships, legal issues, and a changing business environment:

1. Brilliant Ascent to Wrestling Stardom: The narrative starts with Sytch's brilliant ascent to the status of a wrestling celebrity in the vivacious 1990s. She made a name for herself as a charismatic and powerful manager, helping to bring back the heyday of professional wrestling.

2. Shadows put by Personal troubles: When personal troubles put a pall on Sytch's legacy, the story takes a moving turn. Substance misuse problems surface, a bothersome companion that

dulls the shine from her once-dazzling wrestling
character.

3. Legal Unrest and the Dimming Spotlight: As
Sytch deals with many arrests and court cases, the
legal unrest casts a deeper shadow. Courtroom
tragedies entwine with the wrestling tradition, and
the spotlight's dimming effect accentuates the
difficulties she encounters both inside and outside
the ring.

4. Erosion of Professional position: As Sytch's
professional position declines, the heritage of
wrestling goes from strength to weakness. Fearful
of the dangers that come with personal struggles,
wrestling promoters turn away, which lowers their
profile and makes them reassess their place in the
profession.

5. Financial hardship and Economic Shadows:
Included in the shadows is financial hardship
brought on by the repercussions of the law.

Penalties, legal fees, and financial ramifications create a shadow of doom and become concrete representations of the larger issues that come with the waning legacy of wrestling.

6. Attempts at atonement Amid Shadows:
Sytch's quest to traverse the shadows via atonement attempts gives the voyage a redemptive turn. Participating in rehabilitation programs is a brave step in the direction of regaining a past clouded by difficulties in one's personal life and complicated legal issues.

7. Legacy Shrunk Outside the Squared Circle:
The implications of a wrestling legacy that has shrunk outside the squared circle are significant. Sytch's journey transcends the ring and sheds light on the shadows that permeate every part of her story, serving as a tribute to the larger difficulties of both personal and professional life.

8. Enduring Spirit Beyond Diminished Shadows:
A resilient spirit manifests itself despite the wrestling legacy's fading. Sytch's journey turns into a tale of resiliency, development, and the unwavering search for atonement—a story that endures despite the obstacles she encounters.

Wrestling Legacy Diminished: The complex path of a wrestling legend whose legacy was shadowed by personal and legal difficulties is captured in Tammy Sytch's Odyssey Through Shadows. This story examines the relationship between achievement and failure, fortitude in the face of adversity, and the unwavering spirit that leads Tammy Sytch through the complex journey of her waning wrestling legacy.

7:2 INTROSPECTIVE THOUGHT

Introspection: Tammy Sytch's Path Within

Viewed through the prism of introspection, Tammy Sytch's adventure is a fascinating trip characterized by the intricacies of self-discovery, tenacity, and the need for redemption:

1. Glimpses of Wrestling Fame in the Rearview Mirror: Seeing glimpses of wrestling fame in the rearview mirror is the first step on the path to introspection. The flashbulb moments in the limelight turn into turning points, making Sytch reevaluate the highs and lows of her brilliant career.

2. Facing the Shadows Cast by Personal Conflicts: Introspection explores the shadows left by personal conflicts. As Sytch wrestles with the effects of these difficulties on her identity and wrestling legacy, substance misuse concerns and the complexities of handling legal entanglements become central themes.

3. Legal Unrest Viewed through the lens of introspection:

The legal turbulence that characterized Sytch's path is the focus of the microscope of self-examination. A courtroom of introspection is created by personal reflection, where the results of decisions and the ensuing legal disputes are examined openly.

4. The Diminishing of Professional Status as a Mirror for Individual Development: The diminution of professional status functions as a reflective medium for individual development. The recalibration of engagements by wrestling promoters serves as a metaphor for Sytch's recalibration, signifying a dramatic change in her life's story.

5. Financial Stress as a Stimulant for Personal and Financial Reflection: Financial hardship may act as a stimulant for introspection on both a personal and financial level. The examination of Sytch's life outside of the wrestling arena becomes more complex as a result of fines, legal fees, and economic ramifications that force a reevaluation of priorities.

6. Efforts to Earn Redemption Through the Inner Growth Lens: Redeeming qualities are applied to one's reflections, which serve as a canvas. Sytch's journey toward recovery and atonement is a story of personal development that represents a deep metamorphosis that remains hidden from the general world.

7. Individuality Reckoning as the Center of Introspection: The reckoning of identity is the central component of introspection. To comprehend and reconcile the many facets of her identity, Sytch must navigate the collision between her wrestling character and the reality of her troubles.

8. Enduring Spirit as the Echo of Reflection: Sytch's enduring spirit echoes the sound of introspection. Notwithstanding the gloom and difficulties, the story turns into an ode to perseverance—a voyage characterized by the unwavering spirit that rises from the depths of introspection.

Introspection: Tammy Sytch's Journey Within masterfully depicts the rich tapestry of an accomplished wrestler's journey within. This story explores the interconnections of identity, atonement, and the lasting spirit that characterize Tammy Sytch's extraordinary journey inside herself, illuminating the complexity of introspection.

7:3 INTROSPECTIVE ANALYSIS

Professional Introspection: The Wrestler's Odyssey by Tammy Sytch

The professional reflection lens reveals Tammy Sytch's wrestling voyage, an introspective trip that traverses the highs and lows of her career inside the dynamic world of professional wrestling:

1. Pinnacle of Glory in the Wrestling Realm: The adventure starts in the 1990s, at the height of wrestling glory. Sunny, also known as Sytch, becomes a compelling character who gains recognition for her adeptness in management and adds to the energy of a time that would subsequently serve as a point of reference for professionals.

2. Changes in Wrestling Dynamics: Professional analysis looks at changes in the dynamics of wrestling. Since the professional wrestling world is always changing, the story examines how these changes affect Sytch's role and fame and force readers to reevaluate her place in it.

3. Exposing Personal Challenges as Professional Crossroads: As professional reflection and personal challenges converge, the story becomes more complex. Problems with substance misuse and legal entanglements develop into turning points that affect not just Sytch's personal life but also her reputation as a professional wrestler.

4. Legal turbulence and the Impact of Public Scrutiny: A major issue in professional thought is legal turbulence. Numerous arrests and court cases expose Sytch to public view, shaping the way the wrestling community views her and adding to the complexity of her career story.

5. Effects on Career Trajectory: This professional reflection explores the effects on Sytch's career path. A decrease in opportunities and a reassessment of her place in the profession result from wrestling promoters recalibrating their engagements in light of the possible hazards connected with personal issues.

6. Financial hardship and Economic Realities: One of the most important areas of focus for professional reflection is the financial hardship brought on by legal ramifications. Fines, legal fees, and economic ramifications shed light on the financial realities that complicate Sytch's career path.

7. Attempts at Redemption and Professional Reinvention: Sytch's efforts to recreate herself take a redemptive turn in her professional reflection. By actively pursuing professional redemption via rehabilitation, she has a strong will to overcome the obstacles ingrained in her wrestling story.

8. Legacy Reckoning and Shaping Future Engagements: Taking stock of Sytch's wrestling legacy is crucial to professional evaluation. She wrestles with the effect of personal setbacks on her professional identity, and the introspective phase serves as a catalyst for forming her future interactions, whether in the wrestling business or not.

Professional Reflection: Tammy Sytch's Wrestler's Odyssey captures the complex path of a legendary wrestler negotiating the complex junctions of personal hardships, legal issues, and the changing professional wrestling scene. This story illuminates the contemplative moments that characterize Sytch's career reflection—a voyage characterized by resiliency, reinventing oneself, and the unwavering quest for atonement within the squared circle.

CHAPTER 8: EFFORTS TO FIND ATONEMENT

Seeking Redemption: Tammy Sytch's Tenacious Journey of Self-Transformation

Intimately interwoven throughout Tammy Sytch's path is a story of redemption attempts—a persistent, valiant effort to overcome personal hardships and legal obstacles, signifying a tenacious quest for change:

1. Recognition of Personal challenges: The story starts with a deep acknowledgment of the existence of personal challenges. Tammy Sytch lays the groundwork for a road of redemption by acknowledging the dark forces that have undermined her once-illustrious wrestling reputation.

2. Making an Effort to Rehabilitate: Sytch makes an effort to actively participate in rehabilitation, which is a manifestation of attempts at atonement. She addresses the causes of her problems in counseling and therapy sessions, looking for insight and recovery in the quest for a changed and redeemed self.

3. Public Acknowledgment and Apology: Making amends and publicly owning up to errors are important steps on the road to restoration. Sytch displays humility in front of the public, apologizing for the consequences of her conduct and resolving to make amends.

4. Accepting Personal Growth Opportunities: Accepting personal growth opportunities is how redemption manifests. Sytch embraces learning opportunities, skill-building, and self-improvement projects both within and outside of prison walls—a demonstration of her will to get beyond her mistakes from the past.

5. Handling Legal Difficulties with Resolve:
Handling legal difficulties with resolve is a
necessary part of the quest for redemption. Sytch
takes on legal challenges head-on, observing court
directives and actively taking part in legal
proceedings to show that it is committed to
responsibility and correction.

6. Seeking Professional Reinvention: Looking for
professional reinvention is another way to try to turn
oneself around. With a renewed dedication to her
art, Sytch hopes to redefine her place in the
wrestling world by addressing issues and
reestablishing confidence with both promoters and
fans.

7. Community Engagement and Advocacy:
Sytch's engagement with the community and his
advocacy for constructive change demonstrates
how Redemption transcends personal borders.
Engaging in outreach initiatives, sharing her tale,

and making charitable contributions become essential components of her story of redemption.

8. Sustaining Sobriety and Mental Health: The path to atonement includes the dedication to maintaining sobriety and mental health. Sytch places a high priority on her physical and emotional well-being, demonstrating a proactive attitude to preserving her resilient and changed self.

The narrative in Tammy Sytch's book, Attempts at Redemption: A Resilient Pursuit of Transformation, is one of resiliency and self-discovery. This thorough examination is a powerful witness to the continuing spirit of human development and change by capturing Tammy Sytch's diverse efforts as she bravely attempts to redeem her story.

Rehabilitation After Prison: Tammy Sytch's Road to Atonement

Tammy Sytch's story of her trip out of jail is a riveting account of her attempts at recovery; it's a chapter that comes to life with fortitude, revelation, and a fervent desire for atonement:

1. Moving from Incarceration to Freedom:

Sytch's move from jail to freedom marks the start of the post-prison story. As she embraces her newfound freedom, she must overcome the difficulty of readjusting to society, paving the way for a profoundly healing phase of recovery.

2. Active Participation in Rehabilitation

Programs: Participating actively in rehabilitation programs is a sign of post-prison recovery efforts. Sytch accepts counseling, therapy, and educational programs as essential parts of her road to recovery because she understands the necessity for personal development.

3. Commitment to Sobriety and well-being: Sytch's steadfast dedication to sobriety and well-being is a key theme in the recovery story. Life after jail serves as a blank canvas on which to prioritize one's physical and mental health, denoting a proactive strategy for preserving a stronger and more resilient version of oneself.

4. Public Apologies and Responsibility: Sincere apologies and responsibility are the first steps toward rehabilitation in the public domain. In a public statement, Sytch apologizes and accepts responsibility for the effects of her previous decisions on both the wrestling community and herself.

5. Professional Reintegration and Wrestling Redemption: Efforts to achieve professional reintegration and wrestling redemption were made during the post-prison era. To regain the confidence of both wrestling promoters and fans, Sytch is recommitting herself to her profession and wanting to redefine her place in the business.

6. Community engagement and Advocacy: Rehabilitation initiatives go beyond individual confines to include advocacy and community engagement. By actively participating in outreach initiatives, sharing her own experience, and advocating for positive change, Sytch adds to the larger tale of recovery and atonement.

7. Accepting Chances for Personal Development: The road out of jail serves as a blank canvas for accepting chances for personal development. Sytch embraces learning opportunities, skill-building, and self-improvement projects, underscoring her will to move beyond the difficulties that defined her background.

8. Handling Legal Responsibilities with Care:
Rehabilitation and handling legal responsibilities with care go hand in hand. Sytch's steadfast adherence to court directives and legal prerequisites demonstrates her resolve to resolve the legal complications that stem from her history.

Post-Prison Rehabilitation Efforts: The book Tammy Sytch's Road to Redemption provides a detailed account of a famous wrestler's trip out of prison. This thorough investigation documents Tammy Sytch's many endeavors as she actively seeks recovery, aiming for advancement on a personal level, professional atonement, and a revitalized sense of purpose outside of prison walls.

8:2 TRYING TO MAKE A RETURN

Seeking a Resurrection: Tammy Sytch's Tenacious Comeback to the Forefront of Attention

The story of Tammy Sytch takes an intriguing turn as she sets out on the difficult path of trying to make a comeback—a tenacious quest characterized by tenacity, self-discovery, and an intense desire to recover her place in the wrestling spotlight:

1. Setting the Stage for Revival: As Sytch prepares the groundwork for a revival, the story of his quest for a comeback begins to take shape. After going through a difficult time, she makes a bold comeback to the limelight by setting out on a quest to take back her place in the wrestling industry.

2. Reestablishing Contact with the Wrestling Community: Making a concerted effort to reestablish contact with the wrestling community is a necessary step in the recovery process. Sytch interacts with fans, other wrestlers, and organizations to mend fences and reassert herself in the complexities of the business.

3. Creating a Redemptive Wrestling Character: The creation of a redemptive wrestling character is essential to the story of the return. By incorporating themes of resiliency, personal development, and the unshakable spirit that typifies her quest for atonement, Sytch aims to reinterpret her identity.

4. Exhibiting professional development: Making a return and exhibiting professional development go hand in hand. Sytch shows development in both her abilities and attitude, exhibiting a revitalized love for her work and a readiness to change with the times to fit into the changing wrestling industry.

5. Transparency and Accountability in the Spotlight: These two elements are important to the comeback story. To change her story in the public view, Sytch is honest about her history, owning up

to her faults and exhibiting a measure of
responsibility.

6. Public Appearances and Fan Interaction:
Making a comeback involves both of these
activities. Engaging in events, conventions, and fan
engagements, Sytch cultivates a feeling of
connection and appreciation for people who have
helped her along the way in her wrestling career.

7. Handling the Difficulties of a Comeback Trail:
The story of making a comeback recognizes the
difficulties that always arise. As she continues on
her journey to recovery, Sytch surmounts doubts
and confronts future roadblocks with fortitude.

**8. Striking a Balance between Personal and
Professional Development:** Making a comeback
requires careful consideration of both personal and
professional development. Sytch aims for balance,
making sure that her return to prominence is both a

sign of her ongoing personal development and a comeback in the wrestling community.

Seeking a Resurrection: Tammy Sytch's Resilient Comeback to the Light captures the perseverance and will of a legendary wrestler who is determined to rise once again. This in-depth examination dives into Tammy Sytch's many endeavors as she maneuvers through the challenges of a return, presenting a striking picture of her relentless quest to retake her position in the wrestling limelight.

conccusion:

Closing Thoughts: Accepting Strength and Salvation in the Darkness

The story of "The Fall of Tammy Sytch: From Pro Wrestling Star to Prisoner" shines a light on a journey characterized by fortitude and the unwavering spirit of redemption as the last chapter comes to a close. The narrative of Tammy Sytch, which was once characterized by the highs and lows of wrestling fame and jail, becomes a monument to the ability of people to change.

Following Sytch's life story, we get to see the touching moments from her early wrestling career, her rise to fame, and the ultimate collapse of her reputation due to personal hardships. The difficulties she has outside of wrestling rings, the legal issues she faces, and the consequences for her career status all play important roles in this intricate story.

Nevertheless, the real meaning of Sytch's narrative emerges in the aftermath of his imprisonment. The individual's efforts at rehabilitation upon her release from jail, her attempts at redemption, and her tenacious pursuit of a comeback all contribute to the picture of a wrestling personality that is characterized by her determination to rise above her circumstances. Reflection from both a personal and professional standpoint reverberates as Sytch negotiates the challenges of identity, sobriety, and mental health.

The last few pages of this book reveal a complex picture, one that is not just about a fall but also a rise, a tale that goes beyond the confines of the wrestling ring and speaks to the universal themes of human weakness, resiliency, and the never-ending quest for atonement.

The attention is not just on Tammy Sytch's wrestling character but also on her path of perseverance as she works for a return. Instead of ending abruptly, the book acknowledges that every setback may serve as a springboard for a victorious ascent and that every shade can eventually give way to the brightness of a newfound purpose.

Ultimately, "The Fall of Tammy Sytch" is not simply a story of decline but also rise; it's a story of highlights and shadows, of struggles and victories, and it asks readers to consider the resilience of the human spirit in the face of hardship.

EPILOGUE: TEACHINGS ENGRAVED IN THE RING OF LIFE: A LEARNED EXAMPLE

"The Fall of Tammy Sytch: From Pro Wrestling Star to Prisoner" concludes with a trip that inspires contemplation on the deep teachings carved in the turbulent rings of life. The painful reminder that Tammy Sytch's journey is full of wisdom and perseverance comes at every turn, every up and down.

The lesson here is not just about the drawbacks of celebrity or the effects of personal adversity, but also about the potential for human redemption. It's proof of the resilient spirit that refuses to let the past's shadows define it. Sytch's journey emphasizes the value of introspection, taking responsibility for one's actions, and the transformational potential of seeking atonement.

The book ends with a reminder for readers to apply these principles outside of the pages, as life is like a dynamic wrestling bout that calls for flexibility, resilience, and a never-ending quest for improvement. The story of Tammy Sytch acts as a mirror for readers from different backgrounds, showing not just the common difficulties and victories but also the traps of the wrestling world.

The epilogue serves as an invitation to reflect, to take lessons from both the highs and lows in Sytch's life, and to acknowledge that each setback may serve as a springboard for a more promising and redemptive future. Beyond the boundaries of a wrestling story, the teachings etched in life's ring provide a universal tale of hope, change, and the never-ending pursuit of a return, both within the squared circle and in the larger fabric of our tales.

REPERCUSSIONS: TAMMY SYTCH'S EFFECT ON THE WRESTLING World

The story of Tammy Sytch, which is detailed in "The Fall of Tammy Sytch: From Pro Wrestling Star to Prisoner," has a profound effect on the wrestling world and transcends beyond the squared circle. It changes people's perceptions, sparks debates, and leaves a lasting impression.

1. Thoughts on Vulnerability and Tenacity: The wrestling community considers the vulnerability of its stars and the tenacity needed to overcome personal obstacles in response to Sytch's narrative. Her story serves as a mirror for both spectators and wrestlers, encouraging compassion and empathy.

2. Reevaluation of Industry Pressures: The book makes one reevaluate the difficulties and pressures that come with working in the wrestling business. It starts a dialogue on the toll that stardom can have on people, emphasizing the necessity for mental health programs and support networks within the wrestling community.

3. Legal Scrutiny and Accountability: Talks about legal scrutiny in the wrestling community center on Sytch's legal troubles. The story opens up a conversation on accountability by highlighting how people in the field must handle legal intricacies with care and responsibility.

4. Effect on Career Opportunities: Sytch's problems have caused ripples in the wrestling world, making others reevaluate how personal hardships might affect professional prospects. In light of these issues, promotions and other wrestlers would find themselves having to make judgments about involvement and cooperation.

5. Redemption Stories and Second Chances: The story encourages the wrestling community to have conversations about redemption. Sytch's road to recovery and his efforts at return provide opportunities to reflect on the way the industry views second chances and the possibility of redemption stories.

6. Heightened Awareness of Personal Challenges: Within the wrestling community, Sytch's narrative brings attention to personal challenges. It acts as a trigger for recognizing that people with genuine, often difficult struggles are hiding behind glamorous personalities, highlighting the need for compassion and assistance.

7. Advocacy for Mental Health and Rehabilitation: The book influences the wrestling community's advocacy for programs related to mental health and rehabilitation. By focusing on the members' well-being, Sytch's attempts at post-prison rehabilitation catalyze the development of a more encouraging atmosphere.

8. Ongoing Discussions about Industry Evolution: The influence of Sytch contributes to ongoing discussions over the development of the wrestling business. It raises questions about the need for ongoing adjustment to the shifting dynamics, stressing the significance of dealing with one's obstacles and adopting a culture of development and resilience.

The wrestling community is at a turning point in its history as a result of Tammy Sytch's journey—a chance to examine, grow, and change. The influence goes beyond only recounting the tale of one person; rather, it encompasses a larger story of development, accountability, and the wrestling industry's shared duty to mold the careers of its stars.